Spooky Valenti[ne]
COLORING BOOK

Danielle Cottontail

COLORING BOOKS

Hi, my name is Danielle

I AM A GRAPHIC DESIGNER AND I LOVE COLORING BOOKS. I ENJOY COLORING WITH ALCOHOL MARKERS, AND THE BOLD & EASY STYLE IS MY FAVORITE! FIND ME ON TIK TOK "DANIELLE COTTONTAIL" AND SEE HOW I PAINT MY COLORING PAGES

THANK YOU FOR SUPPORTING MY SMALL BUSINESS. YOUR PURCHASE MEANS SO MUCH TO ME AS I CONTINUE MY JOURNEY ON AMAZON, FROM THE COMFORT OF MY OWN HOME. I WOULD BE VERY HAPPY TO SEE HOW YOU COLORED THIS BOOK. PLEASE SEND ME A PICTURE OF YOUR WORK IN THE REVIEW SECTION ON AMAZON, ALONG WITH A SHORT OPINION AND YOUR THOUGHTS ABOUT THE COLORING BOOK.

I hope this coloring book brings you as much joy as it brought me to create it!

Amazon Selection Paper is excellent for colored pencils. I chose it due to the lack of other options for black-and-white printing. If you use alcohol markers, place an extra sheet of paper underneath to prevent color bleed-through. Test the spread of colors on a separate sheet to avoid going outside the lines. Water based markers are not the best for this type of paper

Enjoy!

FOLLOW ME ON TIK TOK

FOLLOW ME ON AMAZON!

Swatch your colors!

COLOR SWATCH

Printed in Great Britain
by Amazon